SAFE
AS
HOUSES

FROM SOLDIER TO PROPERTY MILLIONAIRE

SAFE
AS
HOUSES

STEVEN GREEN

STEVEN GREEN
Property Investment Academy

ISBN: 9781796218466

Independently published by Amazon KDP

For further information, please contact enquiries@sgpropertyinvestmentacademy.com

This work was produced in collaboration with Write Business Results Ltd. For more information on Write Business Results' business book services, please visit our website:

www.writebusinessresults.com
or contact us on: 020 3752 7057
or info@writebusinessresults.com

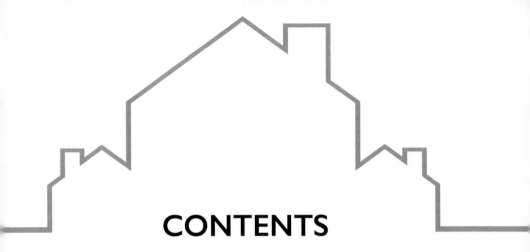

CONTENTS

CHAPTER ONE

SAFE AS HOUSES

There is an old saying which people use when something is a safe choice; maybe you use this saying yourself?

"It's as safe as houses."

I'm sure you will have heard of it? You know if someone refers to something as being as safe as houses then it is deemed a pretty safe bet.

So my question is, why invest in something that is judged to be as safe as houses when you can invest in the actual thing itself?

Most people don't know eight out of 10 millionaires have come from property and the majority of all rich lists are involved in property investing. This demonstrates the potential in property investing and why some of the world's most successful entrepreneurs say property is the best investment you can make.

When interviewed by This is Money, Richard Branson said property was the best investment he had made. He bought Necker Island for $180,000 and in 2006 it was worth $60 million, which is a 33,233% increase. He called it his best financial move.

Did you know Arnold Schwarzenegger made his first million through property? That's right; he actually used money won from his first competitions and invested it into property. He still invests in property to this day.

Warren Buffett, one of the richest men in the world, who also invests in property said: "If you don't find a way to make money while you sleep, you will work till you die."

One thing I've learnt in life is that everybody knows how to work for money but very few learn how to make money work for them. Wherever you are on your property journey, there is an opportunity for you to create a dream lifestyle through property with the right knowledge.

Before we go any further, I want to just tell you that I swear a lot when I speak. While it may offend some people, I do it naturally. I've toned it down for this book, but the odd one might creep in. I'd rather focus on my content and how I can help people. If that means you don't want to hear me speak or keep reading, I'm ok with that.

So if you're still with me, let's find out where you are on your journey.

★ Are you in a dead-end job or one that takes too much of your time?

★ Are you paid well but have to work away and don't get to see your family and children as much as you'd like?

★ Does your job require you to be on standby?

* Is your commute to work too long and you therefore feel like you are forever stuck in traffic?

* Are you sick of being controlled and want to shape life on your terms?

* Or are you fed up of having to watch your money because there is never enough for what you'd like to do?

There was a time when I experienced all of these things. Although I had a fairly decent wage in the Army and I got to see the world, my family time was very restricted and I was constantly driving back and forth to camp over 300 miles each way. I just never felt appreciated and really wanted to shape life on my terms. I knew if things were to change that I had to learn how to make time for what was important and do the things I wanted so I could become financially independent. As much as I'd enjoyed seeing other parts of the country, the time came when I no longer wanted to go away on operational tours.

I had my realisation one night in August 2008, shortly after arriving home from a long day at work.

During this period I was posted just 90 minutes from my house, so I used to commute to work each day. I generally left the house at 6am to get to camp around 7.30am and I would usually get home around 6.30pm.

My partner Gemma and I were renovating our home. This was probably the fourth property we'd renovated in a few years – our friends used to joke that we moved around more than travellers in a caravan. It was tiring working long hours then carrying out work on a night and a weekend. Gemma also had a demanding teaching job and due to us both being tired and working long hours, at times it put a strain on our relationship.

On this particular day, we had been carrying out weapon training so I arrived home around 7pm. Gemma was at the door waiting for me to get home. I could see she looked serious as I got out of the car. I felt tired and thought we were about to have an argument, which I really couldn't face. But then she started to smile, it was a smile that I hadn't seen for a while. Her whole face lit up, and I'll never forget this conversation.

"Guess what?"

"I don't know Gemma, tell me. Have we won the lottery? Or have some magic elves finished the house while we were at work?"

"Nope, come on guess! Do I look happy?"

"Yes you do, I'm not actually sure if I like it. Does it involve me driving somewhere for something for the house because you've had an idea about the wallpaper you want? What is that in your hand?"

"What do you think it is?"

"I don't know. It looks like one of those things Grandma used to stick under my tongue when I was a kid to see if I was poorly or not."

"You're so dumb at times Steven, you make me laugh. It's a pregnancy test."

"That's good, whose is it? What are you doing with it? You're clearly not thinking of having a baby. Are you?"

The day Gemma told me she was pregnant I knew I couldn't go away on operational tour again. There was no way I could write another death letter before we deployed, something we all had to do just in case we were one of those that never came home alive. The feeling I would get writing those letters to my loved ones to read if ever I was to be killed in action was heart breaking. I'd enjoyed parts of my time serving in the Army and learnt some great skills, which have since helped me to help thousands of people all around the country. However, this was when I knew it was time to start creating life on my terms, to build an income that could provide an amazing lifestyle for me and my family.

Property has given me the freedom to choose when I work, what I work on and what days and at what time. When you are doing the things you choose it doesn't feel like work. I enjoy getting up every day. In the last 12 months I've made more money from property than I could have in 22 years in the military whilst having fun doing it. I'm experiencing things now I could only ever have dreamed of. I get to take my daughter to school and pick her up and take my holidays when she has hers. Property has also replaced my partner's wage meaning we all get to take our holidays together. I no longer need to commute to work – I can work from the comfort of my own home.

Now I'd like you to imagine what that would be like for you. All it takes is for you to learn some simple but effective steps which, once followed, will create a dream lifestyle for you too. There are clients of mine all over the country who are making life-changing money with my help.

Let's look at some of the reasons why property is a great investment and what it can do for you.

REASON 1: LEVERAGE

Property is the only investment where banks are willing to put up 95% of the investment value. This means you can get leverage on your money. Let's have a look at what I mean by leverage. For this example we're going to say Paul has £50,000 to invest. Let's say Paul puts the £50,000 into stocks and shares and receives an 8% return on investment. He would receive £4000 profit.

£50,000 / 100 X 8 = £4,000.

Now let's say Paul invests the £50,000 into property and buys two properties at £100,000 with an 80% loan to value, meaning the bank will put in the £80,000 on each property and Paul puts in £20,000 on each property. This would leave him £5000 for each property for legal fees and mortgage fees. This means Paul now owns two properties which are worth £100,000 each, giving him a total property value of £200,000.

Let's say you get the same 8% return on investment as he did on stocks and shares; only he now gets a £16,000 gain. This means he would get 400% more from property because he gets leverage on the bank's money.

Read this again if it doesn't make sense. If you still don't get it, read on. It will start to sink in as you read the book.

REASON 2: SHORT, MEDIUM AND LONG-TERM INVESTMENT

Maybe like me you were led to believe property is a long-term investment? Property can be a long-term investment but you should never view it purely this way as you will massively limit what's possible.

When you purchase property you should look at making money on day one. But you should also look to make money from one of the following as well, medium term or long term depending on your strategy.

An example of a short-term investment would be to buy a property below market value, meaning you instantly make money.

An example of a medium-term investment would be to buy and flip a property after a renovation. Maybe 8-26 weeks from purchase to completion of works and sale of the property.

An example of a long-term investment would be to buy and hold the property to gain from capital inflation.

Top tip: when buying property aim to make money on day one and also make it either a long-term or medium-term investment, depending on whether you're planning on selling or holding.

I prefer to hold my property so I can create a passive income, that way you can build them up creating a recurring income which will allow you to become financially independent. I do occasionally flip properties when I know I can sell them at the high end of market value. If you keep hold of them you can use that income to replace a wage and to give you time and freedom back which I'm sure we could all benefit from, especially when time is just about one of the only things you can't get back.

REASON 3: COMPOUND EFFECT

The day you understand compound effect and take action towards it is the day your life changes forever. A quote that's often attributed to Albert Einstein, although whether he said it is up for debate, sums this up perfectly:

"Compound interest is the eighth wonder of the world; he who understands it owns it, he who doesn't pays it."

I'm going to give an example of a compound that works, showing how momentum is gained and how it just keeps growing faster by the day. See the table below.

Years	Amount	Total	Years	Amount	Total
1	£10000	£11,000	11	10%	£28,531.14
2	10%	£12,100	12	10%	£31,384.25
3	10%	£13,310	13	10%	£34,522.67
4	10%	£14,641	14	10%	£37,974.93
5	10%	£16,105.10	15	10%	£41,772.42
6	10%	£17,715.61	16	10%	£45,949.66
7	10%	£19,487.17	17	10%	£50,544.62
8	10%	£21,435.88	18	10%	£55,599.08
9	10%	£23,579.46	19	10%	£61,158.98
10	10%	£25,937.40	20	10%	£67,274.87

You can see how quickly it starts to gain the momentum. Here's the thing though, we only give this example on £10,000; the average house price in the UK at the time of writing this is £226,906*. Consider how much this would be worth with modest 3-4% inflation.

Now here is the thing, if you understand how to recycle your money you can quickly build up a £1 million portfolio, I'm sure you can see what that would be worth in 20 years' time at just 4%. Yes that's correct, you'd be a millionaire, something so many people think is out of their reach.

It's actually pretty easy to become a millionaire and I know what you might be thinking now.

It looks too easy it can't be right, or it looks too good to be true and if it looks too good to be true it usually is.

We are conditioned to think this way; it's how the majority of the population thinks so it's nothing to be concerned about if you have felt this way up to now. The very important thing to know though is if you continue to think this way you have just killed your dream lifestyle. Remember that old saying: "If it looks too good to be true it probably is." What if this was one of those cases which goes against the grain?

I meet a lot of people who tell me they wish they'd gone into property investment years ago. They tell me they can't believe what I've achieved. The important thing to note with this is I've managed to achieve my success in the most difficult times and things are on the up. I also learnt that if you have a specific strategy you don't

* https://www.gov.uk/government/news/uk-house-price-index-for-april-2018

need to worry about the property cycle, you can create your own cycle of success which we will come onto in the future chapters.

The reality is that property will always be around, certainly our lifetimes anyway and there will always be a demand for people to buy it, sell it and rent it. It is not going to go out of fashion or die off like some of the latest investment fads. The thing I love about property is that you're in charge of how it performs whereas some other investments are controlled by things out of our power. Taking all these things into consideration, you can see why people still use the saying, "it's as safe as houses".

CHAPTER TWO

WHY NOW IS THE TIME

I recall a time in life when I deemed myself to be very lucky. I'd recently returned from a tour of Afghanistan when I was given an opportunity which would change my life forever.

Afghanistan is a very rundown country as I'm sure you can imagine and on the campsite we had very limited amenities. In the Army we were taught to make the best of adverse situations. With this in mind, and knowing we were there for four months minimum whether we liked it or not, we quickly started to put things in place and the priority as always was to make our own gym.

We asked for permission to join two spare tents and set up a weights area. This consisted of water jerry cans full of water for lifting, an Army roll mat, which is designed for sleeping on but which we used for doing our press-ups and sit-ups on, two large sledgehammers for bicep curls and a piece of timber like a scaffold board between two chairs which we used as a bench to train chest press on. The good thing about being a Royal Engineer was that we had multiple tradesmen and a load of hand and power tools. Two Polish guys had managed to bring out some brand-new shiny 20 kg weights so we agreed to let them use our gym if we could use their weights. We used an old metal frame and connected the weights to a pulley system with a rope. After clearing the area of any minefields, we created a 1km running track on the perimeter of our tents.

Like magic we had created our own gym.

For four months two of my good army friends, John and Brew, and I trained every day before work and after work. As I'm sure you can imagine there is very little to do in Afghanistan, so it was either lie on your camp cot for three hours until bed time or go to our gym and train or run. I became fitter and stronger than I had ever been and when I returned to the UK four months later we were given our standard fitness test. Out of nearly 100 guys I came first. I was usually in the top 10% and knew I was in great condition but even I surprised myself.

Later that day, one of our Staff Sergeants walked into the troop store and told us a guy who was well known for his fitness levels was supposed to be going on his physical training instructor's course the next day, but couldn't attend due to an injury. He was looking for someone to take his place on the training course. Normally it would require a lot of physical training to prepare for passing a course of this nature, so there were no volunteers out of roughly 30 guys in the room. Everyone knew the reputation this course had for being a beasting, which in military terms meant getting pushed to your physical limits every day in a strict, disciplined environment.

He asked again and not a soul responded. At this point he told us he'd pick someone if no one volunteered. This particular Staff Sergeant was known as Big John. He was around 6'2" tall, about 40 years old and was a huge frame of a man with hands like shovels. He wasn't the kind of guy you'd say no to.

One guy shouted: "Greeny why don't you do it? You're fitter than us lot. You just came first on that running test the other day." The focus of the whole room was now on me, every guy was looking at me hoping I'd agree so Big John wouldn't pick someone at random. 15 to 20 lads all started saying: "Yes Greeny, why don't you do it?"

Big John turned and looked at me with a glaring stare. I knew I was probably the fittest in that room that day, although I was one of the youngest and I still didn't have any rank. I was at the bottom of the food chain and the course was normally only for Lance Corporals and above, which ruled me out.

"I would do it but I have no rank so I can't go on the training, it will have to be someone who's been promoted to Lance Corporal at least," I said, thinking this would get me out of it.

"Greeny, good, well done young man. Don't worry about the rank I will take care of that. I will get you temporary promotion to Lance Corporal. Your training starts tomorrow, come with me and I'll sort your joining instructions," Big John said. And that was it. When Big John made a decision it was final.

Realising what I'd just agreed to, I was excited but also scared. Eight weeks later, after a very challenging time with beastings every day, I'd qualified and was issued my physical training instructor's (PTI's) badge to sow on my uniform, a very proud moment I must say. Off the back of my new position my confidence grew a lot and I became a well-known name due to being one of only eight PTIs out of nearly 800 men on camp. Due to my new role I was quickly promoted and also offered numerous other training courses like swimming instructor, which landed me a six-month role in the outdoor pool in Cambridge as a pool lifeguard. I also completed mountaineering, rock climbing and kayaking qualifications, as well as spending many more weeks away doing amazing things.

For many years I looked back on the day Big John handed me that opportunity and asked myself how could I be so lucky? There were people who had been waiting two years to get on that course and normally over 100 lads would have been in the store, but around 70 were away that day so missed the opportunity. There had been guys fitter than me who were on other operations and were a lot more suitable for the role. Also, I often asked myself why that other lad had got an injury at that time, gifting me the opportunity by being in the right room at the right time.

CREATE YOUR OWN LUCK

It wasn't until four years later that I learnt we create our own luck. I told the story to a smart businessman who told me the definition of luck is when preparation meets opportunity. He said I'd created my own luck by being physically fit and training hard in Afghanistan and an opportunity had arisen from this. I recall him saying that without that preparation the opportunity wasn't there. I realised he was right and I could see for the first time that I was able to create my own luck in life.

So what does all this mean for you?

As you read this book I'm pleased to tell you that you're preparing yourself, you're educating yourself. You're creating the first element of luck (preparation). Now what if I told you the second element (opportunity) was already present, but you just possibly weren't aware of it? You would then have the two elements needed for luck: preparation and opportunity.

Let me tell you about some of the opportunities available to you right now. Although there are about 10 opportunities, I'm going to cover just three, which will be more than enough to make you realise how important this time actually is for property investors, why now is the time to get involved and how you'd be crazy to miss this opportunity.

Maybe you have heard now is a bad time for investing in property?

It's been in the papers a lot and there's also uncertainty around property which we will cover in this chapter. The good thing is that bad press about property is great for you and me. With a good strategy like my own step-by-step system, The Millionaire P.R.O.P.E.R.T.Y M.A.P, you can really take advantage of this great opportunity in front of you.

Firstly let me tell you a little about why property is getting bad press at the moment and how we can use this to our benefit.

You may have heard about the changes in tax related to property or you might actually be experiencing the pain if you own properties in your own name. The big change is what's known as Section 24.

Section 24 was introduced recently and prevents a property investor from being able to offset their mortgage interest, or any other property finance, against their tax bill beyond the 20% basic rate. It essentially removes the higher-rate tax relief available on mortgage interest costs. I want to show you an example of what that could look like for certain individuals.

This has been introduced by the government on a four-year plan meaning:

Year 1 (from 6 April 2017) you can offset on the first 75%

Year 2 (from 6 April 2018) you can only offset on the first 50%

Year 3 (from 6 April 2019) you can only offset on the first 25%

Year 4 (from 6 April 2020) it will be 0%; meaning none of your mortgage can be offset against the rental income.

If a property investor owned property in his/her name before Section 24 and they had the example of rent and mortgage from below you can see what profit is left. Then see the table below of an example of Section 24 in 2020 when the investor can't offset any of their mortgage costs beyond the basic rate.

For ease of maths, let's say before Section 24 you had a rental income of £6000 PA and the interest on your mortgage was £3000. At this time you would only be taxed on the £3000 profit. In 2020 the same investor will be taxed on the full £6000. You can see why amateur untrained landlords are leaving the market.

Here's the thing though: you aren't going to be an untrained amateur landlord. You are on the journey to learn how the smart property investor can use this to his/her advantage.

Right, let's look at that example in more detail. It's important to know these are rough figures based upon recent tax rates, which can go up and down. It's also not taken into account any liabilities you can offset or any profits and losses carried forward. I am not a tax expert and you must seek tax advice from a specialist. The purpose of this is to show you the potential impact of Section 24.

BEFORE SECTION 24 (AVERAGE UK RENTAL INCOME)

Rental Income	£10908	20% Tax	40% Tax
Mortgage	£8908		
Profit	£2000	£1600	£1200

AFTER SECTION 24

Rental Income	£10908	20% Tax	40% Tax
Mortgage	£8908		
Profit	£2000	-£181.60	-£2363.20

You can see that somebody who was making a decent little profit could now have a liability on their hands meaning it's actually costing them to keep their property. If you own just one house which was costing you, say, £2000 per year you might be able to ride this out, but can you imagine having 20+ properties? The losses could run at £40,000+ per year from just 20 properties, which is not a large portfolio. There are people who own hundreds who are being affected by this.

To add to this, at the time of writing this book there is also a lot of uncertainty around Brexit, which then creates uncertainty in the market. Now as bad as Section 24 looks, there is a way you can protect yourself and that's to transfer your properties into a limited company. The challenge with this is that it triggers stamp duty as you need to sell your properties to a company you own. Due to the properties being sold from you personally to a company; it triggers this tax obligation and some people can't afford to pay the high stamp duty amounts so they find themselves in a Catch-22 situation, making them desperate to sell their properties.

I'd like you to put yourself in the shoes of someone who was making £30K PA through property and it's now costing them money to keep their property. What do you think they're going to need to do?

That's correct; they're going to need to sell as quickly as possible and if they need to sell fast, they're going to have to sell below market value to achieve a quick sale.

This is where your first opportunity comes in.

OPPORTUNITY NUMBER 1: BELOW MARKET VALUE (BMV) PROPERTIES

There's never been a better time in either my or your lifetime to buy as much BMV property as there is right now. I am buying properties as much as 35% BMV meaning I can make £20,000+ the day I complete on the sale and up to £120,000 on day one on my larger projects. Even on the smaller scale ones, it doesn't take many of these to create some real momentum. There are landlords all over the country who are not trained enough to know how to deal with the messy situation they're in and they need out fast. They need people like me and you to help them out. The longer it takes them to sell their property, the more money they will lose and the more desperate they become meaning they have to drop their prices even more.

OPPORTUNITY NUMBER 2: SUPPLY AND DEMAND

Currently the UK target is to build around 300,000 new houses per year, which we're falling short on, and the UK population is continuing to rise, which means demand is outstripping supply. This means that the demand for rental is very high. This creates a number of opportunities within itself, way too many to mention in this book. The main thing to note here though is that there is a huge demand for property meaning you as the investor can achieve good rental yields and have a good choice of tenants.

OPPORTUNITY NUMBER 3: LOW INTEREST RATES

As you probably know, interest rates have been at an all-time low for years. I want to repeat this again and for you to really take in what I'm saying here, even though we have seen a very small increase recently, interest rates are still at incredibly low levels, so what does this mean for you and how can you take advantage of it?

This is pretty basic maths; if you can borrow money at say 4% and turn it into 20% you will see you have a 16% gain. The cheaper you can borrow money, the more profit you can make. As the rates are this low now, there is a high chance that they will never be this low again, certainly not in my or your lifetime, meaning this opportunity will be lost. Experienced investors and entrepreneurs are capitalising on this right now. Five years from now when it's too late, people will talk about this opportunity and how you could get mortgages as low as 1% and personal loans as low as 3%. Just stop for one second to absorb this and look at how you could benefit.

Let's just say Claire has equity in her house. She bought if for £100,000 10 years ago and it's now worth £130,000.

She put down a £10,000 deposit meaning she owed £90,000 and the mortgage was on repayment for 25 years at 3%, so she now owes roughly £61,000.

On a 90% mortgage her lender would let her remortgage the property, meaning she could get 90% of the value. We said this was £130,000, so she could remortgage the property for £117,000

As she only owes £61,000 she could get an extra £56,000 to invest with.

Let's say her interest rate is still 3%, although there are cheaper rates at the time of writing. That means she would pay roughly an additional £385 per month on repayment over the remaining 15 years which = £4620 pa.

This would give her enough money to buy three properties at £70,000 if the loan to value (LTV) was 80%.

Let's look at that in more detail.

If she sourced three properties at £70,000 and had to put in a 20% deposit, she would need a £14,000 deposit for each. This would leave £4,666 on each house to cover stamp duty, solicitor's fees and valuation etc.

I got to this figure by dividing the £56,000 by three, which is £18,666 for each of the houses.

Now let's say her buy to let (BTL) mortgages are 4% interest only and we said she took 80% LTV mortgages. She put in a £14,000 deposit on each, which means she has an outstanding mortgage of £56,000 on each property. Her mortgage payments equate to £2240 pa or £186.66 per calendar month (pcm) on an interest-only mortgage. I'll explain later why an interest-only mortgage is my preferred strategy.

We are going to say she receives £500 per month rent, which is £6,000 pa. This means the annual profit per property is £6,000 rent - £2240 mortgage payment = £3760 profit.

Now remember she had enough to buy three properties so we have £3760 profit x three houses which = £11,280 profit over the three properties.

If she deducts the £4620 (which is the value of the additional repayments she'll make each year after remortgaging her home) from the £11,280 she would be left with £6,660 pa additional income. Even if she had a void period of a few months and some repairs, she would still be around £5,000 a year better off.

Over the remaining 15 years that would be an additional £75,000, based on the figures above, just by making her money work for her.

Now I want you to consider the following, because this is where the snowball effect takes place.

If she was to buy each of those additional three properties BMV of just 20% she would also make herself £15,000 equity on each property, meaning she could gain an additional £45,000 in the first year. After 12 months she could remortgage again to buy another three houses, which would now mean she would have six houses plus extra cash flow and even more equity if she was to buy the next ones BMV as well.

Some of my mentees have built up over 12 properties in less than 12 months using a simple but very effective strategy like this. I have built up over £2 million of property in a single year using similar strategies.

So let's just look at those three opportunities:

★ There is an opportunity right now to help landlords and buy BMV properties with a good strategy like the one we've run through above. With us, you can learn how to have landlords running to you wanting to sell you their homes at reduced amounts.

★ There is a huge demand for property in the UK.

★ There is an opportunity to borrow money cheaper than ever before.

You, my friend, have just created luck. Your preparation is being met with opportunity.

Let's continue to the next chapter and remove the likely obstacles in your way.

CHAPTER THREE

GETTING PAST YOUR OBSTACLES

Something I hear a lot is:

"I'd love to get into property but..."

The dreaded "BUT" is in fact just a limiting belief, something is getting in your way.

The most common obstacles I hear are:

★ I don't have any money or I don't have enough money

★ I'm too young/old

★ What will I do if I need to fix something?

★ Why isn't everyone doing this?

SHOW ME THE MONEY

Not having any money or enough money is actually a very easy one to solve. There are so many ways to get past this hurdle, but

I'd have to write 10 books to cover it all. Let's take a look at a few examples though.

I recently trained a guy who had enough money to carry out training with us but after investing his money he would have been stuck, that's what he told me. I asked him, "If I held a gun to your son's head could you get money if his life depended on it?" He looked a little shocked at first and started nodding his head and said in a loud voice, "Well yes of course I could if that was going to happen." I went on to ask him if he now had more opportunities because of me getting him to think of it in these terms, to which he replied, "No, but I could do it if my son's life depended on it."

And this is the thing. You will only ever get what you're willing to tolerate, when you're no longer willing to accept something you will stop finding excuses. In life we get one of two things:

You will either get results or reasons.

The result you want or a reason why you couldn't do it or couldn't even attempt it. If you want to succeed then you need to stop giving reasons as to why you can't and focus on the result you want. Once you remove all the reasons why you can't then you will be left to get the result you want.

There are a number of strategies in this book alone where someone can get started with very little money; and I'm talking less than £500. It's actually possible to carry out deals with no money at all, which I've done on a number of occasions with some very large projects which have cleared six-figure profits.

WHAT AGE SHOULD YOU BE?

Another obstacle that gets in people's way is their age. Are they too young or too old? In fact neither of these matter either as there is a strategy for everyone. Is it going to be a little harder to get certain mortgages if you're say 18 or 60+ years of age? Yes of course. There will be fewer lenders available but that doesn't mean you can't start. Our youngest member in our academy is 17 years old. We also have a guy who is 63 who is just getting started. The problem is people are too one dimensional and don't look at creative ways to get round these simple challenges.

WHAT TO DO IF THE BOILER BREAKS

Now there's only really one way I can advise you here. F***ing fix it or replace it.

Joking aside, it completely blows my mind how many times I get asked the question: "But what do I do if the boiler breaks?" If you're buying correctly you should be making instant cash flow from your investment which you will hear me say multiple times during this book. If your margins are correct then you'll have more than enough money to pay for a boiler even if you have to replace it.

Another thing you can do is take out insurance, so if something does go wrong it's covered on the insurance policy. Most boilers nowadays have a 7+ year guarantee and will last 10 years. This works out at around £160 per year, based off a new boiler being supplied and fitted for £1600 and lasting for 10 years. This has become a bit of a joke among the mentees and people like to ask me the question when I'm carrying out training, which often gets a laugh. My reply now is always, "F***ing fix it".

Why isn't everyone doing this?

When people first hear my strategies they come up with reasons why they won't work. Once I've quashed all those reasons they often have a quiet moment where they're trying like mad to think of another reason it won't work. When they realise they have run out of reasons, they often ask me the question which makes me laugh:

"So why isn't everyone doing this?"

This is good though as I know the penny has dropped and it's at this point people say right well I need to know more. I find these inquisitive types of people always go on to make a real success of property investing. Some of my high-end clients who I've taught how to build seven-figure portfolios were once the person who criticised me and had the 100 reasons why it wouldn't work. I often joke with them now about where they would be if they hadn't come to that initial training to see what it was about.

YOU MUST KNOW THIS

The reality is the only obstacle in your way is YOU. Remember there is never a lack of resources only a lack of being resourceful. The day you get rid of the heavy bag off your back and make the decision to get out of your own way so you can actually move forward is the day your results will take off. Once you have moved out of your own way you can move forward, but you're going to need a solid strategy so let's look at that in the next chapter.

CHAPTER FOUR

STRATEGY

Knowing what you want is essential to your success. You must have clearly written goals to keep you focused on the direction you want to go. Without this you become what I call a drifter. This is where you will hinder your results and create confusion and a feeling of uncertainty.

Once this creeps in you may get a feeling of anxiety and fear and if you don't control it, then it will paralyse you and you won't take any action. I want you to think of a ship. I'm sure you'd agree that 99% of the time a ship will get to its desired destination. Imagine if we remove the captain and that ship no longer has anyone directing it and it never has a target. It's unlikely it would ever get out of the harbour, and this is exactly the same as a person who doesn't have clear goals. You will drift around and won't stick with anything because you have not made it clear to yourself where you want to go.

Knowing how to set a proper goal is very important and if you miss out any of the steps you will reduce your chance of ever achieving it or you will slow down the process. Learning how to effectively set goals is vital to your success. This is something I teach on my property training programs. Clear goals give clarity, focus, confidence, motivation and much more, which I could write an entire book on alone.

The main thing for you to do right now is to be clear what it is you want. Write the goal down somewhere you can see it daily and read it to yourself until it's completely drummed into your head. Once you know it off by heart don't stop reading it – it's important you look at it daily. Make sure you chunk it down into stages so you can gauge whether you're on track. The last thing you want is to set a five or 10-year goal and realise it hasn't worked out at the end, as that's five or 10 years wasted. You need to know each year if you are on track, that way you will know if your strategy is working and if it needs tweaking.

The best way to do this is look for problems in advance. If you can identify future problems you can look at how to mitigate them. This means you can think of a solution to that potential problem, or challenge as I prefer to call them. This does a few helpful things.

Firstly, it will help you identify challenges before you have them, which will help you find a solution for them before you feel the pain of the problem. Secondly, it trains your mind to look for solutions.

One of the main reasons people don't achieve their goals is that when they face a problem that they weren't expecting, it throws them off track and can often demotivate them to the point they give in. They might have had this amazing dream which they were enthusiastic about achieving, but if something goes wrong and it's not as they had expected then it can create doubt. If the person holds onto this long enough those negative emotions control them into making a decision of retracting or stopping altogether.

FEAR IS THE BIGGEST KILLER OF ALL DREAMS

Once you have tried to identify all the potential challenges and how you will mitigate them, you must forget them.

Your full focus now gets switched to what you want and how you will get there. Sometimes other challenges will arise that you haven't seen but this won't be an issue, because you have started to learn that each problem has a solution. It will give you confidence to search for the solution rather than being paralysed by the challenge in front of you.

CLARITY

There's something you need before you even think about setting a goal and that is a clear vision.

There is a quote from the Bible that says:

"Where there is no vision, the people perish." (Proverbs 29:18)

Even if you take that in its biblical context, meaning a vision of God, it's still relevant. Regardless of whether you are religious or not, someone realised thousands of years ago that if there was no vision then the person would perish. I take that to mean they would not become what they could've been and would never achieve their dreams. They would not tap into that abundance of potential which lies within us all, including you.

This is why it's so important you have a clear vision. Having a clear vision will give you clarity and help you stay focused on what's important. It will give you confidence that you know what you want in life. Without a clear vision you will feel lost, you may even wonder what life is all about. You will get frustrated and change your mind about what you want and possibly a lack of decisiveness will frustrate you. There is a chance you will suffer from anxiety and maybe worry about unnecessary things.

Another common indicator of a lack of vision is that you constantly create negative movies in your head of potential arguments you may have or things that you will say to someone if they say something to you or do a certain thing.

It's all unnecessary noise, it's all negative emotions built up for nothing. It's your mind's way of filling the gap because you're going to do one of two things regardless of whether you like it or not. You're either going to consciously think into a world you'd like or your mind will fill it with fear and doubt, which is another form of visualisation except done in a negative way.

When you hit a challenge if you can remain focused on what it is you want, rather than the thing you don't, you will instruct your mind to look for solutions. The most important thing here is to understand the relationship between your vision, your goals and your strategy. This is one of the main reasons people get it wrong in life and the consequences of getting it wrong could mean a lifetime wasted.

THE BIGGEST MISTAKE I SEE...

When setting a goal it must come off the back of your vision. I've seen and read a lot of material which talks about goalsetting without any mention of vision.

The problem with this is that you don't think about where that goal comes from. It's a little bit like your goal being to get to the top of a 100-storey building. You place your ladder against the 100-storey building and begin to climb. Each day you're working hard to get to the top (your goal) and eventually with persistence you reach the top. But once there you realise it wasn't the building you wanted to climb. You look over to the building in the distance and your dream lies on top of that building, where you can see other people reaching your dream. The dream you had for you and your family.

Now in this case, it's just a 100-storey building which would possibly be a few hours wasted, but imagine you set a goal that took 10 years or even longer to achieve and you wasted it following someone else's goal or someone else's goal for you. This is why we must have a clear vision of what success looks like before we set any goals. You must know your vision and understand that the goals are stepping stones to take you to your dream/vision. The goal is not the end result; it's the vision that's the end result. This is why the vision must come first. You must know where it is you want to go first, then you set your goals and then you create a strategy.

A strategy is the approach you take in order to achieve your goals.

Without a good strategy you are limited; without a strategy at all you have nothing.

Now I want to give you an example. It may seem a little strange, so bear with me. Let's say you're among the first 1000 people on Earth and none of you had any knowledge passed down to you from ancestors or books etc. You look up at the sky and see how beautiful it looks. You set a goal to reach the sky before any of the others. You want to know what's past those things you have learnt to call clouds. You have a goal, but you don't have a clear strategy.

Possibly at first you would try random things. You may attempt to just jump in the air as this would seem the most logical thing to do to get off the ground. Quickly learning you only had the ability to jump so high, you would give up on that strategy. Without a strategy at all you might just keep thinking about how can you get up there but take no action.

Now let's say you had a strategy but not a very good one. You may attempt to climb something like a tree and then jump off to get higher or even use a pole, a little bit like a pole-vaulter. These would both be strategies and would get you closer to the sky than just jumping from the ground; although they are not very good strategies and again you'd only get limited results.

Now imagine someone came along who knew the way to those clouds through experience or who had been taught by someone else who had already achieved this goal. His strategy might be to make a plane or a hot air balloon which would take him there and he would go above the clouds into the sky. You can see how these people had the same goal, but it's their different strategies that determine if they get there. The strategy is the HOW the goal is the WHERE and the vision is the WHY.

Now that was an analogy and just a bit of fun, we all know how to reach the clouds and know it's already been done. This is the same as becoming financially independent and achieving your goals. If you have a good strategy that is proven to work you just need to follow it and you will achieve your goals. However, if you don't know what the best strategies are then you're likely going to guess just like I used to in the early days, and if you guess then you're leaving your dreams to chance. Unlike the bit of fun in the previous analogy this is your life, this isn't a joke! Remember, you don't know what you don't know.

Yes, I believe in making every day fun and enjoying what you do, but to go through life without a proper strategy is deadly and you will pay the ultimate price for it. It may result in a life of unhappiness, a feeling of inadequacy, a lifetime of working for money rather than money working for you. You'll be giving up all your time in order to make money but in the process give up on doing the things you're passionate about or even worse not seeing loved ones and children due to not having time.

He who aims for nothing will most certainly achieve it.

A life wasted, how sad.

The amazing thing is this doesn't have to be you!!!

Today you get to choose. Today you really reflect on what you want and how you'll get there. Today is the day you start to become the best version of you. Can you remember that version of you?

The one who is loving. The one who is caring. The one who enjoys life and is grateful for everything around you. The one with unlimited potential. The one who has been searching for change. The one who picked up this book and put in the f***ing effort to read it because you are destined to change.

Today is the day you step out of your own shadows and start to take back control of your life. Today is the day you learn your WHY. Today is the day you set some goals. Today is the day you start making a strategy. Today is the day you make a decision to achieve all your dreams. You owe it to yourself. Forget your past, the past is the past. Forget your problems and start focusing on solutions. Relight the fire inside you; let's hear the lion inside you. We both know it's in there so let's hear you f***ing roar.

Now I have made that clear, I want you to know I'm here to help you. During my time in the Army I learnt a lot in those challenging situations serving in Afghanistan and Iraq. They taught me how to be focused, self-motivated, disciplined and work to a strategy daily. This helped me to create a clear map for people to follow; a strategy that has been tried, tested and proven to work time and time again. A system that will let you find your inner strengths and give you the same bullet proof mind set I have built. A step-by-step, no bulls**t, easy-to-follow strategy.

Let's look at some strategies to get you started.

Since working on property from leaving school, I have met some very successful property investors. I've also met those who had no idea at all and I've seen a lot of people make a complete mess of property investing. The thing which surprises me is that I can count on one hand those with a good strategy, those who had a vision of what success looked like and clear goals and a solid strategy for how they would get there.

I believe a good investor should have a diverse portfolio as this is a much stronger model – if there is a change in legislation and you only have one method of producing income you could find yourself in a sticky situation. In my portfolio I have a number of single let houses, which I call my foundation properties. Single houses of two and three beds are always in high demand and you can be selective and rent your property to a nice family, set up a direct debit and you may only need to do an inspection once per year.

I have had quite a few of my tenants for over 10 years. They've kept the property to a very high standard and paid their rent religiously by direct debit or standing order every month and on time. I have never had a two or three bed house empty for more than a few weeks in the whole time of letting out properties. So what should you look for when buying single lets and what is the best strategy?

COMMON MISTAKES

Firstly let me tell you what's not good because this is the approach of most untrained landlords and it's the same approach I had in the early days. Knowing all the things I do now; from years of costly mistakes and weak strategies; I'm able to teach you how to avoid making the same mistakes I have. Here are three of the common mistakes untrained landlords make:

1. Purchase new houses

2. Wait until property prices increase before they remortgage

3. Put their properties on repayment mortgages at the wrong time.

Here's what's wrong with each of these approaches.

BAD APPROACH NUMBER 1: PURCHASING NEW HOMES

Buying new homes is not good because you are going to pay premium prices and this will make a huge difference to your profits. Developers aim to get the best possible prices, which is good for them but it's not good for you as the investor. If you can buy one which requires a little work you will have the opportunity to make money by increasing its value. Also, older homes are generally cheaper to buy per square metre. Another benefit of buying from an individual rather than a national developer is you can get creative with the way you structure the deal. An example of this would be to agree a delayed completion where you could carry out any renovation works between exchange of contracts and completion. There are a number of ways you can get creative which I teach on our training courses and it's very unlikely that a national developer would entertain options of this sort.

Now don't get me wrong, new-build houses are stunning and I've even bought one myself in the past, although I paid over £40,000 less for mine than others did for the exact same house using techniques I've learnt over the years. Remember this is a business and it's not about ego and telling others your entire portfolio is made up of new-build houses, because here's the thing, would you rather have 10 nice new houses that made little or no profit or 10 older homes that give you enough income to never have to work again?

The first property I bought was a fairly new home. It was a two-bedroom bungalow and I paid well over the odds for it. Five years down the line, due to another mistake, I was forced to sell it £11,000 less than I bought it for. I will talk about that later to prevent you from making the same costly mistake.

BAD APPROACH NUMBER 2: WAITING UNTIL PROPERTY PRICES GO UP SO YOU CAN REMORTGAGE AND RECYCLE YOUR DEPOSIT

This one is very common and another mistake I made. Here is the main reason this approach is flawed: if you had £100,000 and you put it down on four houses, say a £25,000 deposit into each, you now have four houses. The problem with this is that you are now out of liquid cash for more deposits, so you have no other choice but to wait until property prices increase.

Depending on where you buy in the property cycle, you might have to wait 10 years until there's enough of an increase to be able to remortgage and get your money back out to enable you to buy again. You are pinning your success to the rise and fall of the property market when there is no need.

If when you purchase you know what to look for and can buy below market value (BMV) then you can make money on day one and you are able to remortgage the property and recycle your deposit and buy again.

This was another mistake I made and I paid the price for it as I completely tied up all my money and couldn't move forward for a number of years. The most frustrating thing was I was spotting lots of good properties for great prices and I had to watch them slip through my hands due to not having any money for the deposits.

It's important that when you buy, you get yourself a property at as low a price as possible. A great way to check this out is to go on the Land Registry website and look at sold prices on the same road. Do your homework to make sure you have bought for a price lower than the others have sold for.

This one approach can speed up your results by years and enable you to build a much stronger portfolio. It also gives you a margin, so if property does drop and you need to sell you won't have lost money as long as you bought it low enough in the first place. We will discuss property rises and falls later and if you follow my strategy it wouldn't matter if property prices fell by 50% or even more.

BAD APPROACH NUMBER 3: PUTTING YOUR PROPERTIES ON REPAYMENT RATHER THAN INTEREST ONLY

Now it's very important you read this slowly, and even read this chapter two to three times so you are very clear on what I am saying and what I am not saying.

Your biggest threat in property investing is cash flow, or a lack of cash flow. Let me explain why. This also covers the part in the last point where I said it doesn't matter if property prices drop by 50%, as long as you get this one thing right.

The huge mistake I made (yes another one) was to be equity rich but cash poor. What do I mean by that? Well let me explain.

I built up a portfolio of around 10 houses between 2006 and 2010 and I had over £1,000,000 worth of property with around £300,000 worth of equity. All my mortgages were on repayment mortgages because I viewed property as a long-term investment. I never realised you could make money short term too. The problem with this was my rental just about covered the mortgages and in some cases I added a little in out of my own pocket. This was fine at the time as I wasn't spending all my wages so I had additional money left over.

However, in 2010 I left the military and I was now making my income through buying, renovating and selling property. By this time I had learnt to buy at BMV prices but I wasn't prepared for the next challenge and this was to be the biggest one that I would face. It's also possibly the biggest challenge I've ever faced in property investing.

Initially everything was going well and I was buying two properties per year which I would renovate and sell, making around £15,000-

£20,000 each time. The property market was still very much in a recession and there was a lot of uncertainty, so getting properties to renovate was becoming very difficult as people were sitting on their homes and not selling. The major problem this gave me was that when a property that needed renovating became available there was a swarm of people fighting over the same property and this often pushed the prices up. This had a big impact on my profits and they dropped to as low as £8000 per renovation which was no longer enough to cover my outgoings.

I was struggling and I still had the added pressure of needing to add money into my rental properties to make up the shortfall between my rent and the mortgage payments as the mortgage payments were higher than the rent I was receiving. Once my reserves dwindled I was in a bad situation and needed cash fast. Although I had a £1,000,000 portfolio and over £300,000 in equity, I was in trouble and my only option was to sell something quickly.

The issue with needing to sell fast is that you will have to sell at a competitive price. I placed one of my properties on the market but nothing was selling and I had to accept an offer which was £6000 less than what I had paid for the property. This was a bitter pill to swallow but I needed the cash fast. I had completely run out of spare funds and bounced on two mortgage payments. I was desperately trying to get the sale over the line and then things got even worse because the buyer came back and said they couldn't get the full mortgage amount, so unless I could drop another £5000 they couldn't go ahead.

Initially I said I was not willing to reduce by that amount, but after reflecting for a few days I had no other choice and had to go back to them and accept a further £5000 off the property. This was a total of £11,000 less than what I bought it for.

Looking on the plus side, which I always try to do, I had spare money and I had learnt a very valuable lesson. It didn't matter I had a portfolio that size and that I had all that equity. A lack of cash flow had crippled me and I learnt that cash was king. I needed to change my model to one where I had a passive income where I no longer had to add money into my properties. I decided that from that day on I would have my properties pay me rather than me paying them.

I needed to sell some more properties and replace them for ones which would give me a monthly return. It was at this point I also realised that having my mortgages on repayment had been too much of a strain and I changed them all over to interest only. This instantly gave me around £200 per month per property, giving me over £2000 per month in total.

I had done this to get out of the situation but it made me realise that not only could property be a long-term investment, it could also be a short-term one and give me a wage to live off meaning even if I never flipped another property or worked again I had enough to live off from the rent; especially if I could raise that to £3000 a month as that would match my wage from the Army.

Now you might be thinking there's a problem with putting them on interest-only mortgages, you will never pay off the properties; because this is what I thought at first too.

UNTIL...

I had a lightbulb moment and realised I could pay off 10% per year without incurring any early repayment charges. This meant I could have the income if I needed it but I also had the flexibility to chip off the mortgage with any additional money I had leftover. From that difficult time I took a lot of lessons and I started to build up my passive income. I realised I could decide what amount of income I would like in order to live the dream lifestyle for me and my family and with anything above this I would start to pay off my mortgages.

There is something very, very important to remember here: you must have a plan to pay off your mortgages. You absolutely cannot be irresponsible and leave them on interest only forever as there will come a time when the mortgage company may not want to lend to you due to your age.

This was the strategy I adopted:

All my properties are on interest only and they were until I reached an income of £250,000 per annum. Once at this point I started to put my properties on repayment mortgages and pay them off. Until you reach a figure you can live off, the money is better in your bank as you always have the option to chip off additional capital if you don't need the money, just check the terms with your lender. If, however, you overstretch yourself like I did by having the mortgages on repayment, you have no choice and if you have a difficult time with cash flow then that could be the difference between you needing to sell a property below market value like I had to, or having that income to live off.

Most of the big national companies in business like Woolworths and Blockbusters that have gone bust in recent years did so because of a lack of cash flow. I worked out that if I had a good cash flow coming in each month then it never mattered if the market was to go up or down. As long as I didn't need to sell, and as long as the cash flow was high, why would I ever sell and get rid of an asset that is constantly going to pay me money for the rest of my life?

The previous strategy of buying and flipping properties was good when the market was increasing but became a very bad strategy when prices started to drop. My success was governed by the fluctuation in the market; whereas with my new adapted strategy which was reaching an income I could live off, I never needed to worry about it.

Because here's the thing, if you had say £100,000 profit per annum from rental would you be that bothered if your portfolio dropped in value by say 10 or 20%? You wouldn't need to sell and why would you want to sell your golden goose? You wouldn't, so fluctuation in the market wouldn't affect you.

Here is another thing.

Over the last hundred years there have been a number of recessions but what's happened to property in the end?

It has always recovered to its original value and then increased to a higher value, just like it has after the recent recession we've gone through. Most people don't know this, but property prices are at an all-time high.

I'd now started to find properties that could give me an instant return and I wanted to know how I could build on this even more. Through attending training courses, reading books and investing in myself I came across the ultimate cash generator known as a cash cow. It was the HMO.

CHAPTER FIVE

HMO

After getting into cash flow difficulties and learning that property could and should pay you money short term both from buying below market value and giving an instant cash flow, I learnt how to increase my income to the next level.

HMO means house of multiple occupancy. This is a property rented out by at least three people not from one household but who share facilities like a bathroom or kitchen.

The benefit of an HMO is that you can have multiple incomes from one. I started looking for my first one around the time I was forced to sell my bungalow £11,000 BMV to prevent me from going bust. I told an estate agent I was looking for an HMO and they said they would let me know if one came up.

I decided to sell a few more houses to free up some cash to reinvest into something that would give me a higher cash flow. This time I was in no rush though, so I could put the houses on for a price I was happy with. As the properties had good tenants I decided I would sell with sitting tenants, so the tenant was able to stay in the property which they were happy about and I still had rent coming in.

A few weeks later the estate agent called me to tell me there was an eight-bedroom HMO that already had a licence going on the market. It sounded exactly what I was looking for. I arranged to view it straight away and I made an offer the same day. After a little bit of haggling we agreed on £118,200. That was the easy bit; the challenging part was that I needed to put down 50% because I had no HMO experience. I now know ways around this, but unfortunately at the time I didn't have that knowledge.

The HMO was very dated and needed a lot of attention. When I bought it, it had four sitting tenants. The great thing was that my interest-only mortgage payments were only £275 per month and the building was producing a good income even off just the four rooms.

Room 1 £75 per week
Room 5 £75 per week
Room 6 £65 per week
Room 7 £65 per week

A total of £280 per week, which is £1213.33 per calendar month (£280 x 52 weeks divided by 12 months).

I might be teaching you to suck eggs here by breaking down that calculation, but I often see people multiply the weekly amount by four, which doesn't give the correct monthly figure.

You can see just from having four rooms occupied I was clearing almost £1000 per month profit. After renovating the property I was able to fill the other rooms. I was able to increase the rent to £90 for one of the rooms without upsetting the tenant, because he had been looking to move into somewhere more modern. The rest were small rooms, so I kept them the same price and renewed the tenancy. After all works to the building I had the following income:

Room 1 £90 per week
Room 2 £85 per week
Room 3 £90 per week
Room 4 £85 per week
Room 5 £75 per week
Room 6 £65 per week
Room 7 £65 per week
Room 8 £65 per week

A total of £32,240 pa or £2686.66 per calendar month, minus my mortgage payments, gave me an annual income of £28,940.

As you can see, a HMO can be a very profitable purchase. I was clearing more than the UK average income from a single property. Having this extra income was a massive weight off my shoulders; I now had enough income to live off my rental properties. This was an amazing feeling, although I never got too excited as I had heard that HMOs could be more challenging than single lets. The issues I'd heard landlords having with HMOs were the same ones over and over again, but I saw this as a good thing as it said to me that this was probably the full list of challenges that HMOs brought and if I could find a solution to each of these I'd pretty much have it nailed and running smoothly.

COMMON ISSUES WITH HMOS

★ Tenants come and go often

★ Tenants fighting over shared fridges and food going missing

★ Shared bathrooms not being kept clean

★ Difficulties splitting electric and gas bills

★ Problems with tenants losing keys and getting late night calls

★ Condensation and damp problems due to high occupancy levels or people drying clothes in their rooms

★ High bills due to lights being left on all night

★ People not locking the main entrance door when leaving and the building not being secure

★ Chasing up payments for multiple tenants and trying to catch them all at the same time.

Once I established what all the main complaints were, I began to look at ways I could mitigate them. During my time in the Army I'd learnt how to solve problems in a systematic way, and I knew as long as I used these skills I would be able to overcome any challenges. Here is how I approached each of the challenges I'd identified.

TENANTS COMING AND GOING OFTEN

I knew that this was going to be one of the main challenges, but I also knew I had to make my HMOs somewhere nice where people would want to stay. As the property was in a rundown condition, it was no surprise to me that people were coming and going often.

The first thing I did was redecorate, getting rid of all the horrible dated woodchip on the walls. I removed all the old bathroom suites and old carpets and gave the whole place a facelift. I renovated the whole property to a high standard and even dressed the rooms, meaning I put beds in each room with a nice duvet and big chunky pillows on the beds. I painted the rooms in nice, neutral colours and fitted some mirrors, which made the rooms look light and larger in size. I put a new hard-wearing blue carpet up the stairs and new carpets and lino in each of the rooms.

TENANTS FIGHTING OVER SHARED FRIDGES AND FOOD GOING MISSING

One good thing the previous landlord had done was putting kitchens within the rooms. This meant each tenant had their own individual kitchen and fridge. He told me that he used to have a lot of problems with people taking each other's food until he decided to get small kitchens fitted in each room. That saved me a problem to address, but I still took out the old dirty kitchens and replaced them with modern-looking cream gloss units.

SHARED BATHROOMS NOT BEING KEPT CLEAN

The next problem to address was the bathrooms and ensuring they were kept to a standard which all the tenants would be happy with. As I had a lot of experience in the building trade and renovating properties, I went for nice-looking tiles in the bathrooms. It's fairly common practice to put in cheap, small white tiles, which in my opinion look cheap and nasty. You cannot expect to get good tenants if you are going to put the minimum into the property. The main thing to note with this is that the difference between a nice tile and a cheap white one could be as little as £60. A well-tiled bathroom should last a good 10 years, so it is crazy to try and save £6 a year over those 10 years.

I also installed some new signs in the bathrooms saying, 'please keep these bathrooms nice and tidy or I will be forced to get the cleaner in more regularly and therefore will have to increase rents'. This has always been enough to ensure the tenants keep these areas clean and tidy.

OUTSOURCE TO ACHIEVE MORE

I have a cleaner who goes to my HMO once every two weeks, her role is to hoover the communal areas and give the bathrooms a wipe over. I've always found when a property is renovated to a good standard and you can educate your tenants into keeping communal areas clean then having a cleaner visit every two weeks is more than enough.

DIFFICULTIES SPLITTING ELECTRIC AND GAS BILLS

The challenge relating to the electric and gas bills is fairly simple to solve. I had individual meters installed for each HMO room. These meters can be installed by an electrician and cost me £140 each with fitting. They come with individual cards, which the tenants purchase from you. I prefer the £5 ones. The way I manage this is to nominate one tenant to look after £50 worth of cards at a time and I used to sell these to him for £45, meaning he got his electricity free of charge for looking after the cards.

PROBLEMS WITH TENANTS LOSING KEYS AND GETTING LATE-NIGHT CALLS

I also gave this tenant the responsibility of looking after the spare keys to each flat. Obviously if you are doing this it needs to be somebody you can trust. I would suggest testing them with the electric cards at first and as that relationship builds you can then give them the keys to the other rooms. I moved somebody into the property that I knew I could trust so I instantly gave him the task of looking after the electric cards and spare keys.

This killed a couple of birds with one stone. I no longer had an issue with electric bills and the property never had gas installed, which I prefer to stay away from. This also mitigated the potential problem of tenants losing keys and calling me in the middle of the night. I explained to the tenants that if they were to lose the keys and I needed to replace them there would be a £10 charge. I gave the task of getting the key cut to the nominated tenant, who was happy doing this as it rarely happened and I also paid him £5 for the inconvenience of getting them a spare key. The key was generally around £4 to cut, meaning I was never out of pocket and neither did I have the hassle of dealing with the situation.

The tenants were fully aware that if the nominated tenant wasn't in they would need to call a locksmith just as anybody else would if they had lost their keys. I can honestly say that I have had less than five keys go missing in the whole nine years I have owned my two HMOs.

CONDENSATION AND DAMP PROBLEMS

I knew I was going to have to deal with potential damp problems caused by people drying clothes in rooms. With my experience in the building trade and being qualified as a damp proof technician, this was a fairly simple one to solve.

I installed humidity tracking extractor fans in each room. The great benefit of these types of fans is that they will continue to run while the humidity levels are high, unlike standard fans which are often on a timer with the bathroom light. I always recommend purchasing a good quality humidity tracking fan as it will be worth its weight in gold. Then I made a small area where I placed a washing machine and dryer that my tenants could use. I had the electrician install a meter which charges them a small amount for each use. I only charge £1 for a cycle as I want to keep it cheap to encourage them to use the machines. If you make the charge too high, the tenants will not use them and you are left with the same problem. The £1 is more than enough to cover the electric and upkeep of the washing machine. Both the potential damp problems were sorted by these two simple measures.

HIGH BILLS FROM COMMUNAL LIGHTS BEING LEFT ON

I'd read on a lot of forums that wasted energy was a huge problem. In the communal areas I had lights installed that were on sensors to stay on for two minutes at a time, which is more than enough for someone to leave their rooms and get out of the main door, and saves the expense of lights being left on all night.

BUILDING SECURITY

The issue with the main door not being secured is also very easy to solve. I had the mechanism changed to a self-closing lock, which means once the front door is pulled closed it automatically locks and you can only get into the building by using the key. This type of mechanism is great as you don't need the key to open the door if you are inside, allowing a quick escape if there was a fire. All main entrances should be fitted with a thumb lock rather than a key lock, and this is the same for the main doors to each flat allowing the tenants to easily escape the building in case of a fire without having to search for keys. This is very important and something you must comply with when being a responsible landlord. It's also something that will be checked by your local HMO officer.

DEVELOPING RELATIONSHIPS

Through experience, most people tend to avoid the council, but personally I find as long as you don't try to cut corners and you do things the correct way the council can actually be a great asset to you rather than somebody you battle with. My local HMO officer is very helpful and is willing to give advice if I pick up the phone and ask him any questions. At the end of the day he just wants an easy life and would rather his landlords were proactive than reactive. Your local HMO officer has a responsibility to keep tenants safe and I'm sure if you were in his or her role you would do the same. If you have questions about what you need to do to make your HMO compliant I'd strongly recommend making a connection and taking the advice first hand from your HMO officer rather than listening to the bloke in the pub. This will save you a lot of potential problems and you also have the peace of mind of knowing you have somebody there for support.

CHASING PAYMENTS FROM MULTIPLE TENANTS

This is not a difficult problem to solve. When I took over my property I told my tenants to set up a standing order and I also collect all payments on the same day of each month. This makes it very easy to manage and to check if any payments are late. Another suggestion, and one that I have used on a number of occasions, is to tell your tenants you are about to increase the rent; however, any tenants who set up a standing order can keep their rents at their current price. This is more than enough to motivate them to set up a standing order or direct debit.

As you can see, most of the problems which landlords have with HMOs are easily solved with some simple systems, treating your tenants with respect and giving them a nice home to live in. Once I get the building to a good standard and these measures are in place I only need to spend one hour per week on my HMO. If you currently own a HMO and spend more than a few hours a week on it, then it is down to your lack of systems and the way you are approaching your property business. A saying that my old mentor used to tell me was, "treat it like a hobby and it will cost you like one; treat it like a business and it will pay you like one".

This is important, so remember it. Too many people treat their properties like a hobby rather than like a business. Remember to build that relationship with the local HMO officer, get them out to visit your property and advise you on the health and safety elements, which may include things like fire alarms, HMO licenses and regulations on room sizes.

Ensure you have the correct insurance in place which is specific for your HMO and choose your tenants carefully. You are always best having one or two empty rooms rather than accepting someone who could become the bad apple in the cart and upset your good tenants. If you ever get a tenant who is upsetting the other tenants within the HMO then I would remove them as quickly as possible. On the few occasions I've had to move tenants out, it's always been resolved in an amicable way. I've always found that if you speak to them with respect and make them aware they are causing problems for other tenants; they are usually willing to work with me or to find another place.

If you treat someone the way you would like to be treated then that's often enough. You also need to be firm. Firm and friendly works best, with clear expectations. I always tell my potential tenants that the building is quiet and everyone respects each other and if they want to party and have friends around then this is not the building for them. If you fail to be clear from the start then you will have potential problems and I believe this is one of the main reasons that landlords have problems with their HMOs.

As long as your HMOs are run correctly and professionally, you will have happy tenants and your HMOs will pay you handsomely. My two HMOs pay me more than my whole military wage did and they take no more than a couple of hours per week to run.

When you have HMOs run correctly you can see the potential they have and also what they can do for your cash flow. There's also something else I'd like to talk about in the next chapter to show you how to make additional cash flow, as this is something that I use on a regular basis. If you get this right then with no more than two to three hours per month you can comfortably make £3000 profit per month.

Let's take a look at deal sourcing.

CHAPTER SIX

DEAL SOURCING

If you want to get involved in property and both time and lack of funds are your stumbling blocks then deal sourcing is the ultimate strategy for you.

WHAT IS DEAL SOURCING?

Deal sourcing is an excellent way to make additional money. It is something you can set up very quickly with only a few hours of work per month and you can comfortably make £3000+ per month.

This is a very effective way to generate instant income meaning you could quickly replace an income you may have from a job. One of the main things I found with property investing when I started is that you quickly learn your local market and as a result I found more deals than I was capable of handling. I would often be tied into renovation projects and see great deals come up but I wasn't in a position to buy so I had to reluctantly walk the other way, or at least I thought I did. It wasn't until I had been investing in property for about 10 years that I thought about doing something about it. Over the last five years my portfolio has been growing year on year and it started to bring me a lot of attention, to the point that people started asking me for help.

WHY IT WORKS FOR LANDLORDS

I found that it wasn't just beginners wanting to know how I was sourcing such good deals and getting the results I was; it was also very experienced landlords with large portfolios. This is when I realised how good I had become at finding deals, pricing them up and turning them into very handsome profits. I was asked by a very experienced landlord to find him some deals to help build his portfolio. Ian was someone I knew from the Army and someone I knew I could work with so we both agreed a deal. I found a couple of deals which were pretty good, but I was determined to find him something that was exceptional so I played the waiting game and eventually I came across a great opportunity through one of my contacts. It was an old solicitors building which had once been two large semi-detached houses. After using my negotiation skills I managed to agree £85,000 for the whole building.

I had plans drawn up for three self-contained flats and three shops below. The deal was superb and Ian now makes around £12,000 pa and he made around £80,000 equity. For this deal I charged him £5,000, which was very low for a deal with these kinds of returns. When you keep your focus on your client and they get a great deal they will come back again. Too many people who deal source only think of their own needs and this creates a very short-lived relationship. I like to work with a small group of serious investors who are in it for the longer term and offer a comprehensive service where we pretty much take care of everything. This can include recommendations of accountants, brokers, arranging plans, managing the property plus much more. Then I have some properties I source and just pass over doing very little work. I charge less for these types of deals because only a very small amount of time goes into them.

KNOW YOUR STRENGTHS

It's a good idea to match your strengths to your services. For example you might have connections to a builder so you can manage any building works, or you may own a property management company where you can take care of their properties for them. On our training programs we work with our mentees to find their strengths and help them put the best package together for their clients.

It's amazing how many people don't see their own strengths and think it's not possible for them. You might think that's you and if it is I challenge you to look deeper. Maybe you're well organised. This is a great strength to have when deal sourcing for clients. Perhaps you have good attention to detail; again this is another great strength. It could be that you are an honest person or hardworking and these are also great strengths that you can fit into a very successful deal sourcing business. When setting up some other points to take into consideration are:

★ Where to find potential clients that you can find properties for

★ What services you will offer

★ Creating contracts for you clients

★ What location you will find properties in

★ What type of properties will you look for and will you have a variety?

★ What price range they are looking for.

WHAT SORT OF FEES CAN YOU CHARGE?

Depending on the quality of the deal and size of the property and its income I generally make between £2500 -£7500 from a single deal; sometimes this can be sorted with a few hours' work maximum.

There is no longer any need to pass up your unwanted deals. You can simply package them up and sell them on. There are literally 100s of ways like this that you can make yourself an additional income through property. When you send the deal to your client make sure you lay it out in a way they can understand and that demonstrates why this deal is worth paying for. Once you have done this you can decide your payment options and again there are a number of creative ways you can do this. For example, you can take your fee on completion of the deal or you might take the whole amount up front, which is a great way to earn instant cash and create a positive cash flow.

When I have needed to generate cash quickly to complete a large project I have sourced deals and offered a discount for upfront payments. On numerous occasions I've generated over £10,000 in a day and as much as £20,000 plus.

If you're going to take payments up front you need to deliver on your promise, so remember to always keep your clients' needs as your main focus and it will always come back to you.

On the deals where I charge £7500 plus, I aim to make my clients at least double this in their first year alone; and certainly to make their full fees back in year one. They will then make profit every year and are sure to come back to you to carry out more deals for them.

GETTING STARTED WITH DEAL SOURCING

When working out the return it's important you don't give out guaranteed returns because you need to be qualified or regulated to do this. It is fine to give an approximate estimation on rent though i.e. low case £400 pcm, medium £450 pcm, best case £500 pcm. I will show my clients a guide based on what is on the open market; that way you are being transparent and I encourage them to check the prices themselves too. This shows you have done your homework but mainly it puts the onus on your client to make the decision.

Even for my clients where I carry out the full package I still insist they look over the deal and make the final decision. This is the best way to maintain a healthy relationship as both parties know exactly what is happening at all times.

When carrying out deal sourcing I consider the following things:

★ Exactly what my client is looking for, in terms of the size, price range, location, and type of property

★ What services I will offer and how much I will charge for each level of service.

Once you know what you will offer then create a contract based on your services. Consider how you will find your clients and what options you have. There is no need to spend any money on this at all; you can use display boards outside your house or even social media like Facebook.

You just have to decide your best strategy for sourcing your deals and there are a number of creative ways to do this. I literally have people contacting me all the time offering me BMV properties and I have clients ready to pass the deals on to.

If you would like information on deals we receive BMV you can get more information on the website at www.stegreen.co.uk.

I'm sure you can see why I love deal sourcing and it's one of the strategies that has allowed me to create multiple streams of income. It can be set up very quickly with literally a few pounds.

Now let's look at three creative ways you can speed up your results with very little money or no money behind you in the next chapter.

CHAPTER SEVEN

CREATIVE THINKING

In my property investment academy groups we all help and support one another and we share our creative ideas. I've created an environment where we try things out and aim to be as creative as possible. Landlords who are stuck in their ways and use old, dated, traditional methods are putting a cap on what they can achieve. I'm not going to cover all the strategies I use, otherwise this book would be a thousand pages long, but let's look at a few powerful strategies which are very simple to apply and will help you to start generating money through property.

LEASE OPTION AGREEMENTS

The first one I want to talk about is lease option agreements.

A lease option agreement (LOA) is similar to a rent-to-rent strategy, except you have the option to buy within an agreed timescale.

Lease options are a brilliant strategy for anyone with no capital behind them or with bad credit history. Lease options allow you to build a portfolio with great purpose as you need very little money and you can often put agreement options in place a lot quicker than the process of buying.

Lease options are also brilliant when there is a downturn or uncertainty in the property market, as it creates a huge opportunity. There are also opportunities created when legislation changes and people are forced to sell quickly. A recent example of this is Section 24 (see Chapter 2 if you can't remember what this is), where certain landlords are in a situation where their profits have been completely wiped out and where their property that used to make them money is now costing them money, meaning it's gone from being an asset to a liability.

A good accountant who is proactive like my own will come up with a strategy to adapt to situations like these, but some accountants are not even sure of the implications. I've seen studies indicating that the majority of landlords either didn't know about Section 24 or didn't fully understand it. If you're untrained this can mean bad times. If, however, you're switched on you can take advantage of the situation with strategies like lease options. So now is a very powerful time to understand lease option agreements and how you can benefit from them.

A lease option means you can lease a property from the owner and then you lease it to someone else for a higher fee, but you now have the right to buy at an agreed price, also known as a strike price or exercise price. The good thing with lease options is you're not obliged to buy but the owner has an obligation to sell; if you exercise the right. This is often referred to as a call option. A call option is the option to buy assets at an agreed price on or before a particular date.

To put an option agreement in place you only need to put £1 into the deal to make the contract legally binding. If you choose not to exercise your right to buy within the agreed timescale you will lose your £1. This is not a typo either if you are thinking that can't be right, surely you can't agree to secure a price for a house and only put in £1.

Yes it's true. Here's another great thing about LOAs: let's say you agree on a £100,000 purchase price and you agree to pay in 10 years' time. If the property increases in value to £150,000 the seller must sell you the property for the agreed £100,000. Remember you don't have to buy, but the seller is obliged to sell.

So now you are probably thinking why would anybody agree to that? Let me tell you.

Let's say Andy owns a property which he bought for £100,000, for ease of maths, and because of a downturn in the market it is now only worth £90,000 so he can't sell the property. His mortgage payments are £250 per calendar month interest only. He's decided he wants to move in with his partner but doesn't want to lose his £10,000 deposit that he put into buying the house. He isn't interested in renting it out and dealing with tenants. So you offer him a LOA, where you will cover his mortgage payment of £250 a month and agree to give him £100,000 in five years' time. This means he doesn't lose his £10,000 deposit and doesn't lose £250 a month by leaving his property empty. He also doesn't have the hassle of selling his house or worrying it's stood empty and may become a target for break ins and his insurance being void due to no one living in it.

There are literally thousands of scenarios where someone would benefit from a LOA. My advice is always give the owner their options even if that isn't the best option for you. This could mean advising them how to rent it out themselves or asking whether they've considered putting it up with another estate agency etc. If you keep your focus on your clients' needs it will come back to you tenfold, I'm a strong believer in that.

As long as you know you can rent this property out for more than £250 per month then you also create yourself a positive cash flow. Let's say you can rent this property out for £550 per calendar month; this would mean you have a positive cash flow of £300 per calendar month. This would give you £3600 per annum, but out of this you would have some fees to pay, such as a bit of maintenance, insurance and so on, so let's say you cleared £3000 per annum after your expenses.

As the market starts to rise again the property could return to its original £100,000 value and increase even more, meaning you get to keep the gain on the property. Even if the value of the property doubled; the seller is obliged to sell it to you for the agreed price. Your cash flow will also increase each year – even with just a marginal increase in rent of 3%, you'd get around an extra £200 a year. This may not seem a lot, but after five years that is over £1000 and if you had just 10 properties like this, that would be an extra £10,000 in those five years.

GAINING MOMENTUM

I've seen some people create lease options for terms of 20 years, meaning the chance of the property value increasing is very high. This is where you can gain some real momentum. Let's say you had 10 properties which were all producing you £3000 per annum; you would quite quickly have an income of £30,000 per annum.

CREATIVE THINKING WITH LOAS

Now let's look at another way for you to approach this. You can get even more creative than this and you could split the property into a multi-let where you could rent each room for, say, £250 pcm and now generate up to £1000 per month or even higher. That means you'd have £750 pcm profit. After your fees you could clear over £8000 per annum off a single property. Just five properties like this would create you an income of £40,000 per annum using very little money, apart from legal fees and £1 to structure the deal. If you had 10 properties like this it would give you an income of over £80,000 PA, which would grow each year with a small increase in rent.

You can see how Andy is in a better situation and you also get to make an instant income with the potential of great capital growth. Another option if you don't want to buy the property is to sell the option on to somebody else. Let's say in this case that the property's value went up to £150,000, meaning you had gained £50,000. You could sell the option for £30,000 to somebody else allowing you to make a healthy profit and you would get a quick sale on the option due to the fact that it is £20,000 below market value.

RISKS WITH LOAS

A few of the risks to be aware of are the owner of the building not paying his/her mortgage, which could result in the bank repossessing the property. You can protect yourself legally by putting something in the contract to cover you from this. It is always worth checking that the owner of the building can afford to make the mortgage payments with the agreed amount of rental that you will be paying him or her.

Another potential problem is that you overestimate the value you can rent the property out for, meaning your cash flow is not as high as you anticipated. You could also lose cash flow if there are problems with the house, so make sure the property is in a good condition for letting as you don't want to be left with the problem of repairing a property to ensure it is habitable.

Before agreeing a lease option, always make sure that the property is in an area where there is good rental demand and be aware that if rental demand drops you could be left making the payments to the owner without the rent coming in. This, however, is no different to any buy-to-let property where you would have the responsibility of paying the mortgage.

Another point to note with lease options where I've seen people get caught out: you cannot agree a lease for longer than the length of term which is left on the mortgage, i.e. if the seller had seven years left on their mortgage you could only agree to a call option for a period less than the seven years as the lender will be looking to get their money back at the seven-year point.

TOP TIP

Get yourself a solicitor who has experience of dealing with LOAs. If you play this smart you can get a solicitor to work with you. An example of this would be if the owner was nervous about the whole process, you could get them to sit down with a solicitor who could explain the process to them. A solicitor will be happy to do this if they know they're likely to get the work out of it. It will also reassure the property owner that you're professional and that this will be a solid legal document that will cover them as well as you in case of any potential problems. You can literally agree anything as long as you both agree to it, then a solicitor can make it legally binding meaning you can get as creative as possible.

There is a great opportunity for lease options at the moment with the new Section 24 regulations. A lot of landlords are stuck with properties that are costing them money and you will be able to give them a solution to covering their mortgage payments and agreeing a fixed price somewhere down the line that suits you both.

You can see that lease options are for the creative investor and not the traditional landlord but they're also very simple to do. Anyone can quickly learn this process and make themselves life-changing money regardless of how much money they have or what situation they have with credit. Just make sure you remember this point and get a commercial solicitor who is familiar with lease option agreements. These are very easy to find too; simply go onto Google and search: "commercial solicitors". These are generally the ones who deal with these types of transactions and there will be loads within a short distance of your home. The whole process is even simpler than it looks.

On our training courses we go into more detail about where you can learn how to have estate agents literally running to you with multiple deals by using certain techniques.

DEFERRED CONSIDERATION

Now let's look at another very creative way to make deals work with little or no money or on terms that suit your cash flow.

Can you imagine going into a shop and getting your shopping but asking if you can pay for it six months later? People don't think these types of things are possible but I'm pleased to tell you they are and I use them on a regular basis.

The thing I'm taking about is deferred consideration; let's take a look at how you can use this strategy.

Deferred consideration is a proportion of the purchase price paid at a later date. So how may this be useful to you?

Firstly let me give you an example of when I have used deferred consideration and how this helped me to structure a deal.

In my local town there was a large derelict pub/hotel, which in its day was a very popular place for people to socialise. The building had been on the market with an agency at the other end of the country, and on a few occasions I'd tried to arrange a viewing but found it to be very difficult to deal with this estate agency that was out of the area. There was never anybody available to carry out any viewings and I was constantly told somebody would get back to me but I heard nothing. I was aware of other investors who'd had the same experience.

But while they walked away, my business partner Mike and I got creative. We searched the Land Registry to see who owned the property. It cost us a small fee of a few pounds to find out the owner of the property and their contact details.

When I got hold of Simon, the owner, explained I was interested in the property and asked if it was possible for us to have a viewing, as the agent had been no help. Simon actually told me he was looking for a new agent, but that he'd be very happy to save this hassle if we could agree a price. We arranged to meet the next day to take a look around the property.

To our surprise, the building already had full planning permission to be split into three two-bed apartments and seven one-bed apartments. The agency had not marketed this information; a building of this size (700 m^2) with planning permission should have been valued a lot higher than what it was on the market for.

After looking around the property I knew quite quickly that this could be a very profitable deal. At the time it would be the biggest project we had done to date. Simon was looking for a minimum of £170,000, as he needed the funds for a larger project. I told him that we couldn't stretch to this amount and as he was very keen to get rid of the property I knew there was an opportunity to negotiate. After some haggling, we reached a price of £150,000. Once I knew he was at the lowest figure he'd drop to, I got creative and told him I could pay £50,000 immediately and £100,000 in six months' time.

Initially I think he thought I was joking, but I explained this would give him the £150,000 he needed. What's more, he'd get £50,000 instantly that he could use to help fund his other project. I told him I would get a draft contract drawn up by my solicitor and he agreed he'd consider the deal if I gave him a contract that he could look over with his own solicitor.

I made a quick call and arranged an immediate meeting with my solicitor where she drew up a contract stating that we would pay £50,000 on the signing of the contracts and the remaining £100,000 at the six-month point.

To cover ourselves we agreed that the property was sold and put it into our names and the vendor (seller) was to take a first charge on the property, this meant me and Mike were totally covered as we now owned the building for only £50,000 down. The vendor was also protected as he had first charge on the property. This meant that if we were to sell the property at any point the vendor would get the first £100,000 from the sale just the same as the mortgage company would if you were to sell a house that you had a mortgage on.

With both us and the vendor protected, we could now use the £100,000 to spend on the project to increase its value. As the building was just a shell, the vendor was happy with this as we were adding value to the building and making it a lot easier for him to get his money back if there was a problem.

We also put a clause in the agreement stating that if we hadn't paid the money back within the agreed six months, we would pay a penalty of £500 per month. This gave Simon peace of mind that we would repay his money on time. It also pushed us to complete the deal on time to avoid any additional fees.

We knew that by spending the additional £100,000 on the building this would add around £150,000-£200,000 to its value. The building was valued at just over £300,000, meaning the bridging company were happy to give us 70% of the value of the property which equated to £210,000.

We now had the money to pay back Simon and we had an additional £110,000 to complete the project. At this point the first charge is removed because the £100,000 was paid to Simon, and the bridging company now take first charge meaning we now owe the bridging company the money instead of the vendor (Simon). With the additional funds we had enough money to complete the project and flip it onto a commercial buy-to-let mortgage, getting back all the funds to pay off the bridging company.

A creative structure like this one enabled us to do a project which had an end value of £630,000 by only using £50,000 of our own money. Using deferred consideration helped us structure this deal and it also gave Simon the £150,000 that he needed to complete his other project. Using deferred consideration was a win-win situation for both parties.

When buying properties I often use creative strategies like this one, and I encourage my mentees to use similar creative strategies. We actually have an award for most creative deal of the year at our annual awards night.

OTHER TYPES OF DEFERRED PAYMENTS

Another creative idea, while we are on the subject of deferred consideration, is to look at deferring payments in other areas to help you structure a deal based around your current cash flow and available finances.

An example of this would be to get an architect to do drawings for you and pay him once the funding is released or if you have a good relationship with the builder who has a good cash flow you could agree to 50% of the payments up front and 50% when the project is finished, which you pay out of your profits meaning you can carry out large projects with very little money.

You can see these are very creative strategies and ones that very few landlords are even aware of. If you want to become a successful property investor then learning strategies like this will help speed up your results and provide opportunities out of nothing. This is what I call real property investing. Now let's look at more creative strategies and how you can use other people's money.

BRIDGING FINANCE

I've honestly lost count of how many times people have said the type of claims I make on what is possible with property investing are b*****ks.

I totally get where they're coming from though and I can see how some of the claims I make do appear to be too good to believe. Naturally because of this people reject the claims and lose out on the opportunity. But if there's one thing that separates me from most other property investors it's my creativity. I believe anything is possible and due to that I'm willing to test things that others won't; the more creative you can be in property the quicker you will see results and the more you will have fun investing.

Bridging finance is like a double-edged sword: get it wrong and it will cost you everything you own, but get it right and you will transform your life. If you don't know much about bridging finance you might have the same opinion that I used to have about it. I knew very little other than to stay away as it was bad.

Back in 2011 and not long after I bought my first HMO, I saw a property that I knew was a great price. It was a commercial shop with two floors above which had previously been used as commercial offices. The commercial shop was let to a guy who had been there a long time and wanted to stay in the building. I knew he was a good tenant and his rent alone would cover the mortgage for the whole building plus some profit. Then I would have the additional rent from the two floors upstairs.

My intention was to make two flats from the space above. The whole building was up for sale for around £80,000. I decided to try my luck at £65,000 and to my surprise the agent came back to me and told me if I could come up with £2000 more they would accept my offer and we agreed on £67,000.

I went to a mortgage broker who was good at arranging mortgages for residential homes; I'd been using him for over 10 years. The problem came when I was told it was a commercial building so there were fewer lenders than for standard residential mortgages. The broker suggested we use bridging finance and then flip onto a commercial mortgage. I knew very little about this at the time so when I heard the word bridging my first thought was to stay away from it. I was very reluctant but was told it would be fine as long as I completed the project on time and on budget, which I was confident I could do, so I made the decision to go ahead.

I started the process and very quickly fees were coming at me left, right and centre, a lot quicker than I was used to with a standard mortgage. There were some fees that I'd never even seen before and it felt like there was a fee for everything. Getting the money was also very slow, not what I'd expected. It took so long we hit a point where the vendor said he was accepting another offer unless I hurried up. I was already well over £6000 into the deal at this point and he was becoming frustrated. I'd paid for planning, surveys, application fees etc. Because I didn't want to lose the deal

I agreed to pay a £2000 non-refundable deposit to the vendor to show I was still serious and everything was fine. In reality I was trying to sort this dreadful mess with bridging finance and I was now starting to realise why I'd been told to stay away from bridging finance.

The straw that broke the camel's back was when the bridging company said the application had expired so I had to pay the fees again. I couldn't believe what I was hearing, as it was them that had held up the whole process. After pressure from my solicitor and my partner Gemma, I walked away from the deal and in total I lost around £10,000.

It was a very difficult pill to swallow; I'd lost another big chunk of money because I didn't know what I was doing. It's fair to say I wasn't going near bridging finance ever again.

I remember that day well. I walked out of the solicitors and straight past my car. I didn't want to go home, I needed some time to think and reflect on the huge mistake I'd made. I headed towards the seafront until I reached a bench which faced the sea. It was a cold day at around 5.30pm and there was no one around, just the sound of the sea. I recall putting my head in my hands and wondering how I'd walked into another costly mistake. I questioned why these mistakes kept happening, and whether this was going to work out and allow me to achieve the lifestyle I wanted for me and my family. A thousand thoughts were going through my head.

Eventually I walked back to my car and drove home. I walked through the door and saw my two-year-old daughter Sadie standing there, staring at me as if she knew. Her hair is a light gingery blonde and she has the brightest blue eyes; her face is very pale with little freckles. I just stood looking back at her and I felt guilty, I felt like I'd let her down. I really wanted to create something for the future but felt like I was going backwards. It was one step forward two steps back. Maybe you have experienced this too and you know what that feeling is like?

Although Sadie couldn't understand what I meant, I made a promise to her that I would get this right as a tear fell down my face. It felt like a very lonely time because I didn't have anybody who could guide me and show me how to avoid the mistakes I was making. If I'd had a mentor I could've saved a lot of money and a whole lot of heartache.

Four years later my property portfolio had grown a little but nothing to write home about. I had tied all my money up, which gave me very few options, and my progress was slow at best. I had to do something to get moving and create some momentum, so I started doing research and came across a host of success stories of people who were using bridging finance. I started to reflect on where I'd gone wrong with my bridging finance. With this deep reflection I could start to see some of my mistakes, such as with the type of bridging finance I should've used and the type of company I should've tried to work with. I started to think that maybe I just chose bad products and a bad company. I realised that just like you could get good quality and bad quality electrical appliances, there were also good quality and bad quality bridging companies. I was getting curious again and started thinking I could make bridging finance work. I knew if I could, I wouldn't need to use any of my own money.

The search began and I started to look at all the products and all the companies, but Gemma wasn't going to stand back and watch me lose more money so she studied the finance options with me.

We both developed a deep understanding of bridging finance and believed we knew where we had gone wrong and that we could put it right moving forward. We started to search for a good commercial broker, someone with experience of using bridging finance who could confirm if we were thinking on the right lines.

Once we had the confirmation that we had all angles covered, we began to look for a property where we could structure a bridging deal.

Outside our offices was an old sweetshop which had two floors above which were unused. The building was very dated and had boarded up windows on the first and second floors. I knew it had been on the market for a long time so I went over and started to discuss figures with the owner. I knew I was close to making this deal work so I paid to have a valuation done and found a bridging company that would give me 75% of the market value rather than the purchase price.

The difference between getting a valuation on market value rather than purchase price can be substantial in terms of the amount you can borrow. We will come onto this in a moment. The valuation of the property came back at £123,500; and when the works were completed the end valuation (also known as gross development value or GDV) was £180,000. This was due to it being split into a commercial unit as well as self-contained flats. It was in a great location as it was just off the High Street and overlooked the seafront. I knew rental demand would be high and it seemed like the perfect property to get started with. I found a bridging company that would lend on the market value, meaning I could buy the property and also have the money I needed to renovate the shops.

Now let's look at those differences.

The difference between a bridging company lending on market value and purchase price on that particular building is as follows:

The purchase price was £68,000 so if the bridging company were to lend 75% of purchase price they would release 75% of £68,000 which equals £51,000.

Now if they lend on market value, which they did, they would now loan 75% of £123,500 which equates to £92,625. That meant I had enough to buy the property plus I had the renovation money, without putting any of my own money in.

I made sure the set up was correct and the fees were clearly laid out. I also searched for a product where the interest was rolled up rather than serviced. This meant I didn't have to pay the interest until I flipped onto a buy-to-let mortgage rather than paying the interest each month. Rolling up interest costs can really help with your cash flow. The difference between rolled up and serviced interest, to make it clear, is that rolled up means you pay interest at the end and serviced means you pay monthly as you go along.

We purchased the property and completed the works, splitting it into a commercial unit and two flats. I then had it revalued which came back as £180,000; the same valuation as when it was valued for the bridging. I also managed to get a mortgage of 75% of this figure, so I could completely pay off my bridging finance and pull a little extra money into my company.

We had done it, we had successfully completed a deal without using any of our own money.

Two things happened as a result of this.

Firstly, I knew I could grow my portfolio to a level I chose rather than always being restricted by a lack of funds. This resulted in us adding an additional £1.5 million worth of property to our portfolio in less than 12 months.

Secondly, it had created a real passion within Gemma. She had enjoyed learning about the finance and structuring the deal so much that she decided she was going to leave her job as a teacher and work in the business with myself and her main role would be to structure finance for other people. She studied and became fully qualified and has now partnered up with Chris, the commercial broker who has helped us build our portfolios. Both of them are very creative and passionate about what they do, I have watched them arrange finance for people when they were told by numerous other brokers it wasn't possible. Chris often says there is a finance product for every single situation it's just about knowing where to look and how to structure the deal. A good broker can literally change the game for you on your property portfolio.

Isn't life funny how things turn out? We went from being stuck to Gemma becoming a mortgage broker. At one point in 2016 we had over £700,000 out on bridging at one time. The cost of this was around £100,000 for 12 months. However we made over £700,000 in equity from the money we had taken out on bridging finance.

Moving forward, bridging finance is something that's very much a part of our strategy. It has enabled us to increase our yearly incomes by more than £120,000 in a little over 18 months.

Just remember it's very important to get the setup right if you're using bridging, and I would suggest working with a broker who has property strategy experience themselves and who has personally used bridging finance because they will have a much better understanding of your situation and your needs.

We are coming to the end of the book now but I'd like to cover one more chapter to add even more value to you. This last chapter is the powerhouse; it's the strategy that can earn you over £1,000,000 from a single project. It is by far the most work, but if you learn it the correct way this can make life-changing money.

It's in this area that I believe I am one of the most experienced trainers in the country. I have over 25 years' experience in the building trade and a vast range of qualifications from qualified electrician, fully qualified joiner, damp proofing technician and BPEC ventilation engineer to four years' experience as a plumber and roofer as an apprentice. I also have the largest construction company in my local area which employs builders, plumbers, joiners, project managers, surveyors and we have our own H&S consultant who helps plan our projects and ensures everything is up to regulations. We also work closely with one of the leading architects, structural engineers and principle designers in the country.

Let's look at the powerhouse in the next chapter.

CHAPTER EIGHT

COMMERCIAL TO RESIDENTIAL CONVERSIONS

Regardless of where you are right now on your property journey, commercial to residential (C2R) is something you must be aware of. There's a reason to learn this right now because this is another opportunity which will likely never be as good again in our lifetime.

We will look at this and why just one C2R deal can set you up for life. I'll also go into how C2R can make a big change to your local area whilst raising your profile; it can also be very rewarding.

C2R is as exactly what it says on the tin; it is converting commercial units into residential properties. An example of this would be converting an old pub or commercial offices into a block of flats or houses.

You will find there are mixed opinions on this and those who don't move with the times will criticise this strategy, and I must warn you what to expect if you take this path.

I want to take the opportunity to prepare you for the naysayers and haters because there will be people who criticise any strategy you follow, especially if you have success with it. This is one thing you have to be prepared for with property investing, with the right strategies you can make a lot of money and the critics will come out of the woodwork. The key thing to remember is that what someone thinks about you doesn't matter. The more successful you become, the more you will have people attempting to bring you down, so you must become thick skinned and learn to stand guard at the door of your mind. You have to stop giving a s**t what other people think and just concentrate on what you are doing.

So now I have prepared you, let's look at why now is the golden opportunity.

Everyone knows that the pub trade has been hugely affected and that drinking in pubs is not what it was 10+ years ago when every pub was bursting with people even during the week. More pubs have closed in recent years than ever before. I'm not saying some pubs aren't thriving, I'm just saying pubs in general aren't as busy as they used to be. This has forced some pubs to close their doors and the recession also hit some businesses hard, which means office spaces and commercial units have been left vacant. Some high streets look like ghost towns and empty rundown buildings are an eyesore, have suffered break-ins and cost public money due to police call outs. All of this can also affect the value of neighbouring properties or can prevent new businesses from starting up.

This is why there's such a big opportunity right now to bring these old buildings back to life, to help prevent crime in your area, to create jobs and to provide a good standard of property at affordable prices. The UK has a real problem with supply and demand, which I mentioned in a previous chapter, and the government are offering incentives to developers to bring these buildings back to life and to convert them into residential properties.

The UK is building nowhere near enough houses to match the growth of the population. From a personal perspective, it's also very rewarding turning old, derelict buildings into nice looking properties and playing your part to help ease the supply and demand crisis.

The good thing for you is that you can buy commercial units for less than you could actually build them for. Let me give you an example of some of the recent buildings I've bought and compare that to my experience in the building trade and what it would have cost to build these projects at today's prices. You will find it very difficult to find a builder who can build a property or extension for less than £1000 per square metre and this would mean finding the cheapest areas in the UK and finding a builder who is not VAT registered, which is very difficult even if he's not doing a great amount of work. The most likely price it will cost for labour and materials would be around £1400 +VAT per square metre. Now compare this to the last three projects I have bought.

Type	Size	Purchase Price	Price Per SQM
Old pub/hotel	700 sqm	£150,000	£214
Old commercial building	431 sqm	£55,000	£128
Old gymnasium and nightclub	2200 sqm	£210,000	£95

As you can see, the prices I've purchased these properties for are incredibly low and the land alone would sell for more than what the land and building cost. This is the reason why some developers knock down buildings, then sell the land on for more than they bought it for with the building. It can be hard for some people to grasp that the land can actually be worth more without a building on it.

YOU MUST BE THOROUGH

When looking at commercial buildings you need to do your due diligence checks first. What I mean by this is certain checks to ensure that the building is suitable to convert.

1. Always check access to the project as you will have a lot of deliveries and you will need a lot of skips for the deconstruction phase.

2. Get your solicitor to check if there are any restrictive covenants which may prevent you from making certain changes to the building or land.

3. Check if the building is listed. A grade 2 building isn't too bad; however grade 1 listed buildings have very strict build requirements to preserve the look of the building. This can require specialist companies and also specialist materials which can both be very costly. It could also prevent you from carrying out certain work which may prevent you from converting the building.

4. Always check if the building has been registered for VAT as this could be a nasty surprise. If a property is registered for VAT it means you'll have to pay the 20% tax on the purchase. It's one that I've seen a lot of developers forget to check and only find out once they have paid for a lot of fees.

5. Check if the property is subject to a Section 106 levy. Local councils will sometimes add a levy charge to larger developments; this is to cover the maintenance of roads and new schools etc due to the increase in properties you're creating. These fees can also differ depending on your local authority but can add a substantial amount to the development costs. I'm aware of developers that have negotiated this fee with the local council and have had the fee reduced to make the project viable.

Those are just some of the checks you need to carry out, but that isn't an exhaustive list.

PROTECT YOURSELF WITH AN OPTION

When I put an offer in for a conversion I put an option in place to cover myself. As an example, on my last project I put down £10,000 to secure the deal on condition that my plans were accepted and I can get my money back if planning was not accepted. If you pull out of the deal for any other reason than what you have agreed then you are agreeing to lose your deposit. This demonstrates that you're serious to the vendor, but it also prevents you getting stuck with a building that you can't get planning on. All due diligence should be done prior to you putting down your deposit.

BUILDING WORKS

When hiring a building contractor there are a lot of things you must do to make the project run in a professional and efficient manner. This is something I go into in great depth on our training courses, but let's look at some of the main things you need to consider. When getting quotes for works ensure you get three quotes. This will give you a good idea where the price should be and you can compare the prices of three different contractors. There is a more advanced way where you can personally dictate the prices, something we discuss on our training, but for now its best you just stick to this method as it's simple but effective.

When selecting a builder ensure he is capable of carrying out your project; it's advisable you ask what experience he has. You can also ask for other evidence, such as pictures of their work and testimonials. You should also ask if they have the relevant guarantees and insurance in place, and I would suggest that you always have a written contract that clearly lays out what works are to be carried out in what timescale and for what price.

Another thing to check for is presentation; i.e. what do their vans look like? Do they look clean and tidy? Do they wear a uniform that's neat and tidy? Are they punctual for your meetings? How do they communicate with you, do they use email rather than a scrap bit of paper? And are they familiar with detailed and itemised quotes/tenders? When working with new contractors I also like to check if they are construction industry scheme registered, and that they have relevant insurance in place.

Once you have got your three quotes and have done your due diligence checks on your contractors, you should also check the following things as part of the contract:

★ What are the payment terms?

★ What type of materials are to be used?

★ How will they update you on progress?

★ Will they use local or private building control to sign off the works? I prefer to use local building control, which is the local council, as I know my team work to the correct specifications, but sometimes builders will use private building control as they may be a little bit more flexible. There is nothing wrong with using private building inspectors, some are very good, but just make sure you are aware who your builder will be using and the reason for that choice.

★ Do they use subcontractors and if so, will they manage them and ensure that they follow the agreed contract between you and the principal contractor? This is the main builder or your point of contact.

★ Be aware of the difference between a quote and an estimate, as a quote will be a fixed price and an estimate means the price will likely move.

I have created some very simple to follow processes that I teach my mentees, which includes things like how to price up your build cost, how to know what a project will be worth once you have converted it, building regulations and how to create a detailed schedule of works.

WARNING

Even if you do not plan to use commercial to residential as your strategy you still need to be very aware of it. The reason for this is because you could be buying a flat in a nice little area which you think will have good rental demand, but then a developer converts a building into a block of new flats right next to your investment which is more modern and competitively priced. This will have an impact on your own business. Another example of this could be one of the large national developers building 500 houses within your local town; you have to consider if this will have any impact on your portfolio. Most often it doesn't, however it is something you still need to be aware of.

Commercial to residential is the powerhouse and carrying out projects which run into the multimillions per year is the reason I find the other strategies very simple. The reason I can get my clients great results no matter what their chosen strategy is that I have vast experience in property investing. Some of my clients have gone from no experience at all to owning million pound portfolios and carrying out large commercial to residential conversions without using their own money.

As we bring this book to an end, you should now have a greater understanding of property development, property investing, why property is a great investment and why now is such an important time. Property investing is the opportunity for you to create a dream lifestyle for both you and your family, just like I have.

SUMMARY

There you have it. Property really is as safe as houses if you have a solid strategy. The things I love about property are that there are so many options that you can get creative with, and you are in control of your own destiny at all times unlike with some other investments.

Although we have covered some great things within this book and I'm sure you have taken things from it which will help you in the future, you have just scratched the surface of what is possible when getting creative. Our training events go into much more detail and teach the most creative strategies to take you to financial independence as quickly as possible.

Thinking without taking action is pointless, but taking action without thinking can be disastrous. With this in mind, make sure your strategy is strong and well planned as failing to prepare is preparing to fail. Read this book several times and learn from my mistakes to save yourself a lot of wasted time and wasted money. The first law of learning is through repetition and the more times you read this book, the more it will sink in. Be very careful of listening to the guy in the pub and following the route of most untrained landlords.

Don't spend your life trying to fit in, when you were born to stand out!

YOUR NEXT STEPS

One of the main things I put down to huge success is actually just small wins every day; consistently moving forward towards your vision is the secret. Too many people think they need to move the world to improve their current position. This is not the case; you just need to start taking action as soon as possible. It's important that you start to think about your vision and what success looks like for you and then set some goals. It's imperative you continue to grow and develop your knowledge further. There was a saying that was regularly used in the Army: "Knowledge is power", but this isn't true. Knowledge is only power when combined with action. Knowledge without action is pointless.

One thing an old very successful business mentor said to me was: "Steven either you pay to invest in yourself or you'll pay twice as much for your mistakes, that's if you're lucky. If your mistakes are big enough then they will completely wipe you out."

There is no need to make costly mistakes or feel alone as we have that covered for you; we are here to teach you the right way and to support you with our training and our very supportive network groups.

You can attend a full day's training at no cost by registering using the link below: www.thepropertyaccelerator.com

I very much look forward to meeting you in person on future training and look out for my second book DISCIPLINE which is the 10 steps needed for success. Without these your progress will be hindered or even worse you will never achieve what you're capable of and deserve.

Love and respect

Steven

WHAT OTHERS SAY ABOUT THE TRAINING AND STEVEN

This course is by far the best course I have ever been on.

This course will give you everything you need to succeed in property from setting your goals, developing a plan to achieve them and using a proven strategy. You will learn more on this course than you can imagine.

I went on this course not knowing much at all about property but always having had an interest and wanting to provide myself another income stream. I left the course massively motivated with a clear plan to reach my goals.

Within 2 months of completing the course myself and another attendee had successfully agreed a deal on a commercial property which will provide us with approx £80,000 in equity, and provide us with an income of £20,000 for the rest of our lives.

This course will change your way of thinking and motivate you beyond belief. Attending this course will also put you amongst other like minded people who will help and support you and that alone is priceless.

My portfolio is close to a million pounds in 12 months and I had no previous experience. I would recommend this course to anybody. It will be the best move you ever make.

Nicky Drury

This is without doubt the best thing I've done. It is truly life changing and I cannot recommend it highly enough. I've gone from no property experience and no knowledge at all to a joint venture and buying a commercial property 40% below market value. It gives you the confidence and knowledge in all aspects of properties and different ways to finance, plus tells you the pitfalls to avoid. With the techniques taught I've managed to secure £150,000 investment. The experience passed on is priceless.

Craig Wallace

A friend of mine told me he had invested in someone called Steven Green - a local property development millionaire. When he told me how much money he had invested, I called him crazy, stupid and naive for months. Then I started to see changes; he was getting involved in business ventures and changing as a person.

This got me curious and instead of talking and judging, I started to listen and learn; I was becoming intrigued.

I decided to invest myself and attended Steven's advanced 3-day Property Investment Academy (PIA) course. My friend had told me that a big part of the course was not only how to invest in property, but also how to look at and change your mindset.

I attended the course thinking I want to learn about purchasing properties and the mindset stuff was interesting but personally thought most of the mindset topics were a load of mumbo jumbo. I couldn't have been more wrong! After attending the 3-day course I became more aware of my surroundings, the people in my life, where my life had been and where I wanted to be. It was now clear in my head and I could visualise everything.

I now keep a journal of my day to day events both personally and for my business, I have started a joint venture with another property developer, I am currently looking at 2 more business ventures also, I have paid off thousands of pounds in debt and learned to control the money coming in / out of my life, and how to invest it wisely.

My family time is more precious and personal than ever, we all take the time to talk and enjoy each other's company more, and although my plan is to stop working away from home, I now smile coming to work.

My life has a whole has dramatically improved since meeting Steven. I have now invested in Steven's 7-day ELITE PIA course, if he can make me more aware as a person from attending his 3-day course so I can change all of the above and I have made triple my money back already, imagine what I will achieve after the 7-day ELITE course. Mine and my family's future has never been so exciting.

Richie Buckworth

I attended Steve and his team's property seminar on Saturday 2nd December. I have to say it was absolutely BLOODY FANTASTIC!!! I loved every minute of it and Steve's honesty, enthusiasm, professionalism and high energy of presentation just cannot help but penetrate your soul.

If you want to get your life, your mind and your finances ship-shape and in positive working order, then Mr Steven Green and his team are the guys for you, I assure you! Many thanks again for a GREAT day.

Simon Wynn

Having been on other property courses where I've invested £30k, no-one teaches mindset quite like Steven. My goal setting skills totally changed. He is the most patient person I've met and will work through calculations and mindset until you get it. Totally genuine and cares about your results. The community support is second to none - you couldn't be in better hands. He is there to literally raise your game. I have no doubt that I'll leave every course I do with added value to my life.

Malveen Jandu

ABOUT
THE AUTHOR

Steven has successfully built up a portfolio of over £5 million consisting of over 70 different properties. This all started with a single BTL property back in 2006. He is the owner of six businesses which between them turnover more than £4 million a year and consist of around 30 employees.

He has been featured on the BBC and ITV and also in his local papers on numerous occasions for his transformational change to his mentees, staff and his local town.

He is an author and multi award winning speaker and has worked with some of the most successful entrepreneurs in the world. He has taught tens of thousands of people how to improve their lives and how to build a passive income, which has made him one of the most sought-after property coaches and mentors in the UK.

He lives with his long-term partner Gemma and their nine year old daughter Sadie. Steven's journey started when he left school and got an apprenticeship in construction before joining the Army at 21. He was involved in construction for a large part of his military career, running large construction projects under high pressure on operational tours where he was awarded three operational medals. During this time he was also involved in teaching, coaching and mentoring all ranks from recruits to highly ranked commissioned officers.

Steven was well respected by both his peers and his managers and was graded the highest possible grades in his yearly appraisals having passed two of the military's most challenging physical courses; the military physical training instructors course and the all arms parachute training where he was awarded the prestigious maroon beret. Steven is very open about how he struggled in the earlier years during certain times on operational tour and how he suffered from PTSD many years after leaving the military. He believes all this played a part in him becoming the mentally strong person he is today.

He continues his passion to help others on their journey, often saying he intends to drag as many people over the winning line with him as possible. If you can see value in being personally coached and mentored by Steven you can enquire at enquires@sgpropertyinvestmentacademy.com. Please note that due to Steven's busy lifestyle 1-2-1 training is very limited and there is no guarantee he will be able to commit.

Property training is run throughout the year and you can find the latest training coming up and claim a free seat by going to the web address www.thepropertyaccelerator.com.

From ourselves and Steven we look forward to seeing you soon at one of our future events.

PIA Team

GET
IN TOUCH

enquiries@sgpropertyinvestmentacademy.com

www.stegreen.co.uk

Book your free place

www.thepropertyaccelerator.com

Printed in Great Britain
by Amazon

43561047R00061